CMPL
WITHDRAWN

THE BERMUDA TRIANGLE
AND OTHER MYSTERIES
OF THE DEEP

WORLD
BOOK

a Scott Fetzer company
Chicago
www.worldbook.com

World Book edition of "Enigmas de la historia" by Editorial Sol 90.

Enigmas de la historia
El Triángulo de las Bermudas

This edition licensed from Editorial Sol 90 S.L.
Copyright 2013 Editorial Sol S.L. All rights reserved.

English-language revised edition copyright 2015
World Book, Inc.
Enigmas of History
The Bermuda Triangle and Other Mysteries of the Deep

World Book, Inc.
233 North Michigan Avenue, Suite 2000
Chicago, Illinois 60601 U.S.A.

For information about other World Book publications,
visit our website at **www.worldbook.com** or call
1-800-967-5325.

Library of Congress Cataloging-in-Publication Data
Triángulo de las Bermudas. English
  The Bermuda Triangle and other mysteries of the deep.
-- English-language revised edition.
    pages cm. -- (Enigmas of history)
Originally published by Editorial Sol 90 S.L. in 2012.
  Summary: "An exploration of why the Bermuda
  Triangle is considered to be a danger to ships and
  planes, and the reality about its dangers; also discusses
  places of actual danger in the oceans. Features include
  a map, fact boxes, biographies of famous writers on the
  Bermuda Triangle, places to see and visit, a glossary,
  further readings, and index"--Provided by publisher.
  Includes index.
  ISBN 978-0-7166-2672-5
  1. Bermuda Triangle--Juvenile literature. 2. Ship-
  wrecks--Bermuda Triangle--Juvenile literature.
  3. Disappearances (Parapsychology)--Bermuda
  Triangle--Juvenile literature. 4. Curiosities and
  wonders--Juvenile literature. I. World Book, Inc.
  II. Title.
  G558.T7413 2015
  001.94--dc23
                                    2015009222

Enigmas of History Set ISBN: 978-0-7166-2670-1

Printed in China by Shenzhen Donnelley
Printing Co., Ltd., Guangdong Province
1st printing May 2015

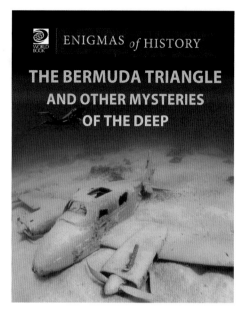

Near the Bahamas, in the Bermuda Triangle, a
diver examines the wreckage of an airplane on
the ocean floor.

© F. Schneider, Arco Images/Age Fotostock

Staff

Contents

The Appeal of a Mystery

The Bermuda Triangle fascinates many people who believe that strange forces may be at work in the region. But, how much is true mystery and how much is sensational legend?

For most of the 1900's, people believed there was something mysterious or sinister about the Bermuda Triangle, a vast region in the Caribbean formed by an imaginary line drawn from a point near Melbourne, Florida, to Bermuda to Puerto Rico and back to Florida (see map on page 18-19). The Bermuda Triangle covers an enormous area of about 440,000 square miles (1,140,000 square kilometers) of open ocean. Over many years, people noticed that what seemed to be an unusually large number of planes that flew over or ships that sailed into the Bermuda Triangle were lost for reasons that were difficult to identify. We all love mysteries because they create excitement and drama in our lives.

But, is the Bermuda Triangle really one of the world's great unsolved mysteries?

The loss of the USS *Cyclops* in 1918 is perhaps the first disappearance that began the legend of the Bermuda Triangle. The *Cyclops* was a *collier ship* (large cargo ship) that set out from Rio de Janiero, Brazil, on March 4, sailing to Baltimore with a load of manganese ore. The ship was never seen again, and all of its crew members were declared lost. Was the ship lost during World War I (1914-1918) to mysterious forces in the Bermuda Triangle? Many authors have focused on this particular event in their investigations.

On December 5, 1945, Flight 19, a squadron of five U.S. Navy bombers, disappeared in the Bermuda Triangle, followed by a seaplane that was searching for the missing bombers. Did the pilots of Flight 19 encounter some unknown force while flying in the Bermuda Triangle? This is perhaps the most famous disappearance highlighting the supposed dangers of the infamous Bermuda Triangle.

Upon closer examination, the mysterious disappearances and sinkings often do have believable explanations that investigators seem to have ignored. Some investigators and authors may have ignored the likely and commonplace causes for the disasters in the Bermuda Triangle in an effort to maintain an air of excitement and mystery about the region. For example, some losses of ships or airplanes in the Bermuda Triangle can be documented as having occurred during bad weather. This area of the Atlantic and Caribbean is prone to frequent storms and hurricanes. In other instances, ships are known to have been carrying dangerous cargo before they were lost.

If the Bermuda Triangle is more legend than truth, are there really areas of the oceans that truly are deadly? Indeed, yes. Some places in the oceans are dangerous because of humans—pirates are a danger in West Africa's Gulf of Guinea, the Gulf of Aden in the Middle East, and several regions of the Indian Ocean. In other places, weather and the geography of the coastline can pose a large risk to ships. The warmer temperature of the Indian Ocean causes dangerous weather patterns, including *monsoons* (strong winds that shift with the seasons) and hurricanes. The weather and ocean currents around the tip of South Africa at Cape Horn lead to unpredictable hazards from icebergs and fierce storms. Ships in arctic waters face extreme temperatures, high winds, and the dangers of being trapped in ice.

Read along and discover why the Bermuda Triangle is infamous, but perhaps not so mysterious. Learn about the dramatic and sad loss of other ships and airplanes. The real story behind the many disappearances of the Bermuda Triangle may seem even more interesting than the manufactured mystery!

BERMUDA

An aerial view of coral reefs near the Bermuda Islands, one of the three points in the Atlantic Ocean that form the legendary Bermuda Triangle.

The Bermuda Triangle

Are mysterious forces at work in this region of ocean where hundreds of ships and airplanes have disappeared?

Some 70 percent of the Earth's surface is covered by water. A view of the globe with the South Pole in the center shows a planet on which continents appear as small islands surrounded by an enormous blue ocean. An observer viewing from a distant planet could easily believe that Earth's surface is completely liquid. From space, Earth appears as a pale blue dot.

The oceans form an otherworld that still holds many mysteries for humanity. Just as plateaus some 16,000 feet (4,877 meters) high and mountain ranges exceeding 26,000 feet (7,925 meters) exist on dry land, a mirror-image of this world on land exists below the surface of the sea. The underwater world has plains 16,000 feet (4,877 meters) deep and trenches that extend far below that. The deepest, the Mariana Trench, has a maximum depth of 36,000 feet (10,975 meters). Conditions in the deep sea are harsh, with icy temperatures, no light, little food, and pressure capable of crushing the *hull* (outer covering) of the strongest submarine. It is a hostile environment, one which shelters creatures whose appearance has fed the imaginations of generations of people fearful of the unknown.

Of the 139 million square miles (360 million square kilometers) making up Earth's oceans, humans have been mostly concerned with sailing on the surface. Knowledge of that aspect of the ocean came from generations of sea explorers. Although humans have been sailing for thousands of years, much is unknown about the Earth's oceans, which remain a source of mystery and wonder. From these mysterious depths, the legend of the Bermuda Triangle rose.

LIKE ANOTHER WORLD

Until well into the 1900's, humankind's attitude toward what lay more than about 30 feet (9 meters) below the ocean surface varied between fear and indifference. The ocean depths have been largely inaccessible to humans for much of history. Fortunately, in recent decades, scientific and technological advances have enabled humans to explore this hostile territory. With the help of such technologies as *sonar* (a device for detecting and locating objects under water using sound) and *bathyscaphs* (deep sea vessels), the ocean floor has been mapped and many of the strange creatures that inhabit the deep have been discovered. Nevertheless, knowledge of the undersea environment

SHIPWRECKS
High shipping traffic in the waters of the Bermuda Triangle, with unpredictable weather, has resulted in a large number of shipwrecks in the area.

is still in its initial stages. In fact, more people have traveled into space than have visited the greatest depths of the ocean. There is so much about the Earth's oceans that we do not know that it is not strange that many areas have high accident rates. There are many things that can go wrong when a ship or airplane crosses the ocean. And, since the oceans are so large, it may sometimes be very difficult to determine exactly what went wrong when something goes missing.

A DANGEROUS REGION

One region of Earth's oceans where things seem to mysteriously disappear is called the Bermuda Triangle. This area stretches between three points: Miami, Florida; San Juan, Puerto Rico; and the Bermuda Islands, a small *archipelago* (island chain) located in the North Atlantic, more than 600 miles (965 kilometers) east of the coast of the United States. In this triangle of ocean covering about 440,000 square miles (1,140,000 square kilometers), several factors interact in ways that may cause problems for ships and airplanes. These variables include a high volume of ship and airplane traffic and, most important, variable weather that can suddenly turn dangerous.

One of the most influential natural elements in this area is the *Gulf Stream,* an enormous "river" within the sea 620 miles (998 kilometers) wide and 325 feet (100 meters) deep. Another is the *Sargasso Sea.* Centered around Bermuda with a surface equivalent to two-thirds of the United States and completely surrounded by a belt of ocean currents that move in a circular, clockwise direction, the Sargasso Sea has been legendary since the late 1400's. It occupies a vast region characterized by prolonged periods of *calm* (no winds). Such a place terrified sailors during the era

of sail-powered ships. At that time, the Sargasso Sea was an enormous graveyard for unlucky sailors. It is precisely these periods of calm and the absence of wind that are responsible for the growth of enormous seaweed forests on the surface of the Sargasso Sea. These forests are populated by what the Portuguese call *sargaços* (sargasso), a seaweed that can grow so dense it makes sailing difficult and even creates the illusion of dry land.

To the south of the Sargasso Sea, the danger is the opposite of calm winds. The North Equatorial Current, returning to the Caribbean from the coast of Africa, heats up as it moves west. The humidity from ocean winds, added to the warmth of the current, generates *hurricanes* (powerful swirling storms) that pound the coasts of the United States, the Caribbean, the Gulf of Mexico, and Central America each year, causing catastrophic damage as they pass.

LOST SHIP
Printed notice (above) about a lost ship posted in the Bahamas in 1974, during the height of interest in the mystery of the Bermuda Triangle.

HURRICANE BILL
An image (above right) of Hurricane Bill, in 2009, as it enters the waters of the Bermuda Triangle between Puerto Rico and Bermuda (the swirling white area in the lower right corner). Fierce storms are common in the region and pose a constant danger to ships.

This complex geographical mix of wind, weather, and sea makes the strongest scientific argument against any supernatural explanations for the ship and airplane disappearances that occur in the Bermuda Triangle. Scientists argue that most of these events result from the many strong storms that occur in the region.

PARANORMAL CLAIMS

Some people who have investigated the loss of ships and airplanes have claimed that many incidents occurring in the region known today as the Bermuda Triangle defy normal explanation and prove that mysterious forces are at work in the region. The disappearance of the crew of the USS *Mary Celeste* is one such example. One hundred feet (30 meters) in length, the *Mary Celeste* set sail from New York on November 5, 1872, heading for Genoa, Italy, loaded with 1,700 barrels of industrial alcohol.

One month later, a British vessel found the *Mary Celeste* drifting with no one on board. The lifeboat was gone, but the cargo and sails were intact. There was no sign of a fire or any crisis that might have caused the crew to abandon ship, and many personal objects were found on board.

The discovery of the *Mary Celeste* was widely reported in exaggerated accounts. Mainstream theories about what may have happened included a mutiny by the crew, an act of piracy, or that the crew abandoned ship out of fear the cargo might explode. However, in the following years many authors, including some who wrote fictional accounts, embellished the mystery surrounding the disappearance of the crew.

Charles H. Fort (1874-1932) was a popular author who wrote about many unusual and *paranormal* (outside the bounds of normal) events, including the strange disappearance

of the crew of the *Mary Celeste*. One of his followers, Vincent Gaddis, published an article in a 1964 edition of the fiction magazine *Argosy*, where he coined the expression "Bermuda Triangle" to describe the area where so many ships and airplanes have sunk or disappeared without explanation. Gaddis's article began with a question: "What is it in this particular portion of the planet that has destroyed hundreds of ships and planes without leaving a trace?"

In 1974, writer Charles Berlitz published *The Bermuda Triangle*, and the mystery of the region was introduced to a broader public. Like Gaddis, Berlitz was influenced by the writings of Charles H. Fort. He also cited the famous American *clairvoyant* (person having the power of seeing or knowing about things that are out of sight) Edgar Cayce (1877-1945) and his fantastic claims about the supposed lost continent of Atlantis. Cayce was very popular in the United States during the first half of the 1900's for his many amazing predictions about the future. In 1940, Cayce predicted that the lost continent of Atlantis would emerge from the depths of the ocean in 1968 near the Bahamas—within the boundaries of what others recognize as the Bermuda Triangle. Berlitz and others speculated that some mysterious technology used by the ancient civilization of Atlantis somehow affected the navigational instruments on ships and airplanes in the region.

FANTASTIC EXPLANATIONS

Another wild explanation for the mysteries of the Bermuda Triangle is the work of *extraterrestrials* (aliens). Outlandish theories claim that aliens patrolling the Bermuda Triangle abduct entire ships or airplanes, or sometimes only take their crews. According to these theories, alien activities are responsible for the many disappearances that leave behind no trace of crews on such "ghost ships." Hollywood film director Steven Spielberg popularized the idea that extraterrestrial activity may have caused many of the disappearances in the Bermuda Triangle in his imaginative film *Close Encounters of the Third Kind* (1977).

Other people think that the Bermuda Triangle may be an area where the laws of physics are somehow changed. Supporters of this theory point to the experience described by pilot Bruce Gernon in 1970. As Gernon was flying over the Bahamas, he reported seeing a kind of tunnel in a nearby cloud. After he passed through, he realized that he had, in just three minutes, covered a distance that would have taken a half hour under normal flight conditions. Gernon concluded that he had experienced a space-time *rift* (break), and that, unlike most pilots experiencing

this, he had returned to tell about it.

The number of unsolved disappearances recorded in and around the Bermuda Triangle caught the attention of the United States Coast Guard and the National Geographic Society. Reputable researchers from these organizations disagree with the theories of Berlitz, Cayce, Gaddis, and Fort.

Other notable *skeptics* (nonbelievers), such as James Randi and Larry Kusche who have examined the evidence, also disagree with the wild theories of Berlitz, Cayce, Fort, and Gaddis, and others who followed. Randi and Kusche pointed out that if an identically sized triangle is drawn in any part of most any ocean, the number of incidents and disappearances would be similar to that seen in the Bermuda Triangle. Kusche found that reports of bad weather were often overlooked by those who proposed paranormal explanations for losses. He also argues that many of the claims about the Bermuda Triangle are outright falsehoods. He points out that the *Mary Celeste* is often included in accounts that investigators attributed to paranormal forces operating in the Bermuda Triangle. This is despite the fact that the deserted ship was actually found closer to the Azores islands, more than 3,000 miles (4,828 kilometers) east of Bermuda.

Today, due to the widespread use of advanced *navigational* (direction finding) technologies, the number of airplane and shipping accidents has declined dramatically. However, even today, airplanes and ships, sometimes even large ones, disappear. Some incidents involving modern airplanes, such as the vanished Malaysia Airlines Flight 370, continue to defy explanation. Such inexplicable disappearances only add to legends about areas of the world's oceans that seem to be cursed or haunted. Such events help to reinforce the legends that surround the Bermuda Triangle.

Vincent Gaddis
(1913-1997)

Gaddis was a freelance writer who first coined the term "Bermuda Triangle." Gaddis used the expression in an article on the topic appearing in the magazine *Argosy* in February of 1964. One year later, he released a book on the mysteries of the sea, titled *Invisible Horizons,* in which he also discussed the Bermuda Triangle.

INSPIRATION Gaddis was inspired by author Charles Fort (1874-1932), who wrote about many paranormal topics.

Larry Kusche
(1940-)

American author Lawrence David "Larry" Kusche, a librarian, trained pilot, and flight instructor, began investigating the Bermuda Triangle in the 1970's. In his book *The Bermuda Triangle Mystery—Solved!* (1972), Kusche concluded that it is a "manufacturered mystery" resulting from poor investigation and occasional deliberate falsification. He has done more to *debunk* (prove false) the claims surrounding the Bermuda Triangle than any other researcher.

MANUFACTURED MYSTERY
Kusche's detailed research shows many losses of airplanes and ships in the Bermuda Triangle have simple explanations.

Charles Berlitz (1914-2003)

A *linguist* (language expert) and the grandson of the founder of the renowned language academies carrying his name, Charles Berlitz is most responsible for encouraging the legend of the Bermuda Triangle. Famous for his many essays on *paranormal* (outside the bounds of normal) topics, including the lost continent of Atlantis, Berlitz wrote the greatest work of his career with *The Bermuda Triangle* (1974), a book in which he analyzed a series of cases of ships and airplanes that vanished in this area. Berlitz examined the official Coast Guard reports and suggested alternative explanations for the disappearances related to extraterrestrials, strange magnetic forces, and the remains of ancient civilizations. The book sold millions of copies worldwide and it firmly established the legend of the Bermuda Triangle. Other authors criticized it severely for the lack of evidence supporting Berlitz's theories and inaccuracies in much of the information presented.

SCIENCE OR SCAM? Charles Berlitz graduated from Yale University and supposedly spoke 32 languages. As a self-appointed expert, he did more than any other person to promote the legend of the Bermuda Triangle.

"In no other area have there been so many unexplainable disappearances as in the Bermuda Triangle."

Charles Berlitz

James Randi (1928-)

James Randi, a Canadian-born former stage magician known as The Amazing Randi, is best known as the world's most persistent investigator and debunker of paranormal claims, including those that surround the Bermuda Triangle. In his book *Flim-Flam! Psychics, ESP, Unicorns, and Other Delusions* (1980), Randi tears apart the idea that there is any mystery about the Bermuda Triangle as he describes the sloppy research by so-called experts on this and many other paranormal subjects. Among the many errors he points out, Randi shows that several of the disappearances supposed to have occurred in the Bermuda Triangle actually happened hundreds of miles away in other regions of the Atlantic Ocean.

PARANORMAL SKEPTIC
A former stage magician, James Randi has spent much of his life disproving the claims of those who state that paranormal forces are at work in the world.

What Is the Sargasso Sea?

This strange region of the Atlantic Ocean figures prominently in sailing lore. It also forms the basis of legends surrounding the Bermuda Triangle.

Christopher Columbus and his crew were the first Europeans to experience the calm winds and waters characteristic of the *Sargasso Sea* on their first voyage to the Americas in 1492. Columbus reported that this sea, which lies partially in a region known today as the Bermuda Triangle, had seaweed so thick it sometimes looked as though they had reached dry land. His crew took depth measurements as they sailed through to make sure that no rocks lay beneath the dense masses of seaweed.

The Sargasso Sea gets its name from *sargaços*, a Portuguese word for seaweed. It is is an irregular, oval-shaped area of the North Atlantic Ocean. No land boundaries mark off this body of water from the rest of the open ocean. It is set apart only by the presence of seaweed that floats on its surface and the *Gulf Stream*, the enormous circular ocean current that runs clockwise around it.

Early navigators who sailed their small ships to North America saw the Sargasso Sea as patches of seaweed that seemed to form sprawling meadows. Many ships were *becalmed* (left without wind for the sails) and sank there. Soon there were legends and myths about the region that told of large islands of thickly matted seaweed inhabited by huge monsters of the deep. Poets and novelists used their imaginations in describing the sea. They pictured

a blanket of netted seaweed from which no ship could escape once it became tangled in the weeds. They described many of the abandoned "ghost ships" as huddled together in a weaving, rotting mass. Shapeless hulks of ancient Spanish *galleons* (large warships with square sails), covered with weeds and barnacles, were pictured lying beneath the waters of this mysterious sea. The passing years contributed skeletons of slave ships, then of pirate ships, and later, the warships of the American Revolutionary War. Wrecks of *clipper ships* (fast, slender sailing vessels) added to the collection after that.

In truth and fiction, the Sargasso Sea is a strange place. By the late 1900's, the Sargasso Sea's reputation as a ship's graveyard was incorporated into the growing legend of the Bermuda Triangle.

SEAWEED
Seaweed that grows in abundance in the Gulf of Mexico is torn free by wind and currents to a section of the Atlantic Ocean where it gathers in huge masses to form the Sargasso Sea.

THE GULF STREAM
This map (above) from the 1700's shows the current's path moving east across the Atlantic.

ATLANTIC CROSSING
An illustration (far left) from the 1800's depicting Columbus's voyage across the Atlantic Ocean.

The Geography of the Triangle

The ocean region bounded by the Bermuda Triangle has a notably complex geography with many hazards to shipping, especially where the ocean shifts from dangerous shallows and sand bars to a depth of 28,000 feet (8,535 meters).

The Bermuda Triangle

The ocean covered by the Bermuda Triangle is subject to a number of very powerful factors that affect navigation in the area.

Sargasso Sea

This North Atlantic region, which lies partially within the Bermuda Triangle, is the only sea that has no coastline. It is characterized by the dense layer of seaweed (called 'sargasso') and by the calm winds that slowed the movement of sailing ships passing through.

The Tongue of the Ocean

With hundreds of small islands, the Bahamas (below) form a shallow platform, divided by a narrow band of very deep water (dark blue) called the "Tongue of the Ocean," which separates the islands of Andros and New Providence.

Gulf Stream

A huge river of water flowing within the North Atlantic from the Gulf of Mexico to Europe. The warm current brings mild weather to Europe.

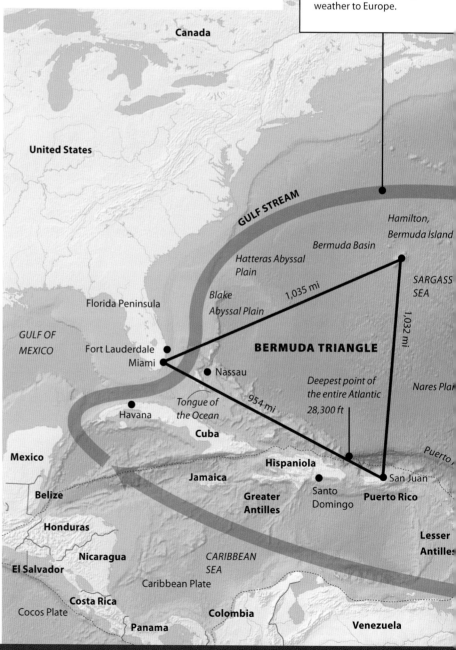

Canada

United States

GULF STREAM

Hamilton,
Bermuda Island

Bermuda Basin

Hatteras Abyssal
Plain

SARGASS
SEA

Florida Peninsula

Blake
Abyssal Plain

1,035 mi

1,032 mi

GULF OF
MEXICO

BERMUDA TRIANGLE

Fort Lauderdale
Miami

Nassau

Nares Plar

Deepest point of
the entire Atlantic

Tongue of
the Ocean

954 mi

28,300 ft

Havana

Cuba

Puerto

Mexico

Hispaniola

San Juan

Jamaica

Santo
Domingo

Puerto Rico

Belize

Greater
Antilles

Honduras

Lesser
Antilles

Nicaragua

CARIBBEAN
SEA

El Salvador

Caribbean Plate

Costa Rica

Cocos Plate

Colombia

Panama

Venezuela

Could Tsunamis Have Caused Some of the Disappearances in the Triangle?

The Puerto Rico Trench, located to the northeast of the island, is the deepest ocean point between North America and the Caribbean. Earthquakes in this very unstable area could cause a giant wave called a *tsunami (tsoo NAH mee)* that could strike the nearest coasts, such as the one that devastated Puerto Rico on October 11, 1918. However, there is no proof that a tsunami caused any of the ship disappearances in the Bermuda Triangle.

Hurricanes

Atlantic hurricanes form off the west coast of Africa and gain strength as they move westwards, over the warm ocean waters.

North America
Europe
Africa

The path of hurricanes

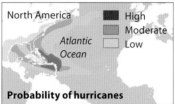

North America
Atlantic Ocean

■ High
■ Moderate
☐ Low

Probability of hurricanes

Sahm Abyssal Plain

ATLANTIC OCEAN

NORTH ATLANTIC CURRENT

The Azores

Mid-Atlantic Ridge

North American Plate

Eurasian Plate

Cape Verde

Cape Verde Basin

CANARY CURRENT

South American Plate

NORTH EQUATORIAL CURRENT

Major Disappearances

Since Columbus first crossed the region in 1492, hundreds of ships and airplanes have disappeared in the Bermuda Triangle. The 1945 disappearance of the five airplanes of Flight 19 is the most famous.

The disappearance of Flight 19

The Grumman TBM Avenger was a torpedo plane used by the United States Air Force and Navy from 1942. A pilot, a gunner, and a radio operator made up each crew. Flight 19 was led by Lieutenant Charles Taylor.

THE SQUADRON'S FINAL FLIGHT

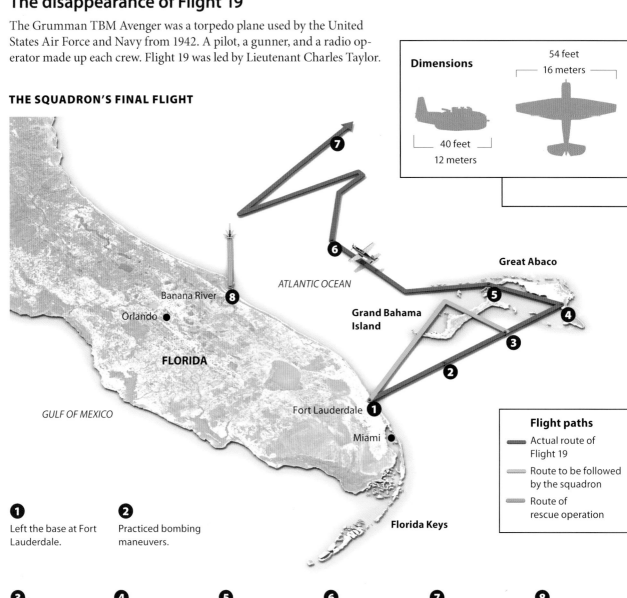

Dimensions

54 feet
16 meters

40 feet
12 meters

ATLANTIC OCEAN

Great Abaco

Grand Bahama Island

Banana River

Orlando

FLORIDA

GULF OF MEXICO

Fort Lauderdale

Miami

Florida Keys

Flight paths

━━ Actual route of Flight 19

━━ Route to be followed by the squadron

━━ Route of rescue operation

❶
Left the base at Fort Lauderdale.

❷
Practiced bombing maneuvers.

❸
Instead of turning northwest at point 3, as was marked on the flight plan, the squadron continued straight ahead.

❹
Taylor confused Great Abaco Island with Grand Bahama Island, which is where he should have been going.

❺
Disorientated, Taylor mistakenly believed the islands he could see were the Florida Keys.

❻
After a chaotic U-turn, the squadron's planes ran out of fuel and fell into the sea.

❼
The likely crash area in the sea.

❽
A Martin seaplane from the base at Banana River, Florida, was sent to the rescue. It exploded in the air minutes after takeoff.

What Caused Lieutenant Taylor's Disorientation During Flight 19?

The TBM Avenger aircraft in Flight 19 had *navigation* (direction-finding) instruments oriented towards the geographical North Pole, not to the magnetic North Pole, as traditional compasses are. Also, all airplanes from that period had two or more additional instruments for orientation, so that if one failed, the pilot could rely on the others. Thus, Lieutenant Taylor's disorientation and his comments about instruments are even more puzzling.

INSTRUMENT PANEL OF THE AVENGER

ⓐ Radio-altimeter
Shows the *altitude* (height) of the aircraft above the ground.

ⓑ Altimeter
Marks the altitude above sea level.

ⓒ Inclinometer
Measures the angle of the wings in relation to the earth's surface.

ⓓ Anemometer
Measures the speed of the aircraft relative to the air moving around it.

ⓔ Directional Gyro
Shows the direction that the plane is heading. It did not work on Flight 19.

Grumman TBM Avenger
It was tough, stable, easy to maneuver, had an excellent radio and remarkable endurance.

Technical Specifications

Empty Weight	10,694 lb (4,581 kilograms)
Crew	3 people
Fuel tank	335 gallons (1,268 liters)
Range (empty)	1,214 miles (1,954 kilometers)
Maximum speed	270 mph (435 kmph)
Maximum altitude	23,400 feet (7,132 meters)

OTHER NOTABLE DISAPPEARANCES

USS *Cyclops* (Mar, 1918)
One of the world's largest freighters sank with 309 people and a cargo of manganese. The Navy called it "disconcerting."

Star Tiger (Jan, 1948) and Star Ariel (Jan, 1949)
The Star Tiger airliner disappeared without a trace. A year later the same thing happened to Star Ariel.

SS *Marine Sulphur Queen* (Feb, 1963)
This merchant ship disappeared in the Florida Keys, with a crew of 39 people and a load of molten sulphur.

The Cessna 172 of Carolyn Cascio (Jun, 1964)
Cascio's last words: "This should be Grand Turk, but there's nothing down there, no airport, no houses... nothing."

A High-Risk Area

Off the coasts of Florida alone, the United States Coast Guard receives an average of 700 calls for assistance from civilian airplanes and boats every month. To this, add a considerable number of military aircraft that have experienced trouble during maneuvers, such as those of Flight 19.

DEDICATED TO ALL U. S. NAVAL AVIATORS
WHO SERVED AT NAVAL AIR STATION, FORT LAUDERDALE
(FT. LAUDERDALE – HOLLYWOOD INTERNATIONAL AIRPORT)
DURING WORLD WAR II

IN PARTICULAR

TO THOSE OFFICERS AND CREWMEN FLYING
FIVE NAVY AVENGER TORPEDO BOMBERS
FROM THIS NAVAL AIR STATION ON 5 DECEMBER 1945
WHO MYSTERIOUSLY DISAPPEARED IN WHAT HAS BECOME
KNOWN AS BERMUDA OR DEVIL'S TRIANGLE.

LT. CHARLES C. TAYLOR,   COMMANDING

JOSEPH TIPTON BOSSI   GEORGE DEVLIN
ROBERT GALLIVAN   FORREST J. GERBER
ROBERT GRUEBEL   WILLIAM LIGHTFOOT
GEORGE PAONESSA   WALTER PARPART, JR.
GEORGE STIVERS   EDWARD POWERS, JR.
HERMAN THELANDER   HOWELL THOMPSON

BERT VALUK, JR.

DEDICATED BY
BROWARD COUNTY WOMENS COUNCIL NAVY LEAGUE OF UNITED STATES
1971

Memorial

A 1971 memorial plaque (left) dedicated
to those lost on Flight 19 mentions the
Bermuda Triangle.

WRECKS Divers and explorers in the Bermuda Triangle are surprised by the large number of ships and airplanes found resting on the seabed.

What Happened to Flight 19?

The case of Flight 19, from Fort Lauderdale, Florida, is undoubtedly the best-known and strangest loss to occur in the Bermuda Triangle.

On the afternoon of December 5, 1945, four months after the end of World War II (1939-1945), a squadron of five Grumman TBM Avenger torpedo bombers took off from the United States Naval base in Fort Lauderdale, Florida, for a routine two-hour training flight. The planes would travel some 300 miles (483 kilometers) on the flight before returning to base. Some 20 minutes after taking off, heading east, the squadron performed the planned bombing maneuvers over some small islands. The planes then were to veer north, and later west, to complete the mission.

However, when the bombers were supposed to be returning, the base received a worrisome message from the squadron commander, Lieutenant Charles Taylor: "Emergency. We seem to be off course. Cannot see land." The control tower instructed him to fly west. However, Lieutenant Taylor's response was frightening: "We don't know which direction is west. Everything is wrong. Everything is strange. Even the ocean looks strange."

Having heard nothing more from the planes in Flight 19, the command center realized that the airplanes had only a few hours of flight time before they would run out of fuel and plummet into the sea. A massive rescue operation involving hundreds of ships and airplanes began immediately. These vessels spent the next three days combing more than 200,000 square miles (500,000 square kilometers) of the Atlantic Ocean and the Gulf of Mexico. The result? Not a trace of the five TBM Avengers. In the course of the search, one of the rescue airplanes, a Martin Mariner seaplane, exploded and crashed shortly after takeoff.

Occurring so soon after the end of the war, the disappearance of this military flight caused a tremendous public commotion. Even though the region where the incident had occurred had not yet been identified as the Bermuda Triangle, people were quick to think the flight's disappearance was beyond explanation. Joseph M. Valentine, a local expert in *paranormal* (outside normal knowledge) events, wrote that the crew of Flight 19 "are still there, but in a different dimension, caught in a magnetic phenomenon that could have been caused by a *UFO*" (unidentified flying object).

Scientific investigators worked to find a logical explanation for the incident. But, even officials in the Navy's investigative committee admitted that the five TBM Avengers "disappeared completely, as if they had flown to Mars. We have no idea

Do remains found in 1991 belong to Flight 19?

In 1991, the remains of several TBM Avenger aircraft were discovered some 12 miles (20 kilometers) off the coast of Florida in approximately 750 feet (229 meters) of water. However, the serial numbers of the airplanes, which were difficult to determine due to the poor condition of the aircraft, did not match those of Flight 19. The airplanes belonged to a squadron lost two years earlier than Flight 19, on October 9, 1943. The solution to the mystery of Flight 19 remains to be found in the ocean depths somewhere off the coast of Florida.

THE TBM'S FLOATING ABILITY

One of the main controversies regarding the infamous Flight 19 was the ability of the TBM Avenger to float. While some authors, including Berlitz, suggested that the plane could float long enough to deploy the lifeboats it carried, others insist that the heavy TBM Avengers would have sunk in a matter of seconds after ditching in the sea.

FAILED RESCUE

Dick Adams (right), a retired Army pilot, examines a map on which the Bermuda Triangle is marked while relating his experiences during the rescue attempt for the five TBM Avengers of Flight 19.

Who Spoke with Taylor?

More than 50 years after the incident, there is a great deal of confusion over the number of people who were in radio contact with Flight 19 commander Lieutenant Charles Taylor. The communication with the control tower is well-established as Taylor describes his confusion before the airplanes were lost. But, were there communications after that? In his best-selling book *The Bermuda Triangle* (1974), Charles Berlitz repeats accounts reported by journalist Arti Ford, in which Taylor seemed to broadcast the chilling warning "Don't come for me... they seem to be from outer space...." No official investigation contains this message, and few Flight 19 researchers believe in its accuracy.

The communication that did occur beyond a shadow of a doubt is that between Taylor and Lieutenant Robert Cox, who was flying in the area that day and heard Taylor's requests for help. Taylor explained to him that he believed he was flying over the Florida Keys, located around 300 miles (483 kilometers) south of his actual position. Cox tried to locate the squadron by sight and guide it to the coast, but did not see any signs of it.

Taylor also communicated with the Coast Guard base in Port Everglades, Florida, south of the air base. The controller suggested allowing another plane from the squadron with functional navigation instruments to guide them, and urged Taylor to switch to the emergency frequency, as his radio signal was beginning to fade from the distance. Taylor, very confused at this point, neither responded nor put these suggestions into action, and continued his erratic path over the Atlantic.

LOST

The members of the squadron lost on Flight 19 pose under one of the Grumman TBM Avengers.

Unknown Causes

The authorities of the United States Navy investigating Flight 19 concluded that the disappearance of the five TBM Avengers was due to commander Taylor's disorientation. However, a few months later, Naval officials reopened the case after admitting that Taylor had been declared guilty without conclusive proof. The loss of the squadron was eventually officially attributed to unknown causes.

Steven Spielberg

This American filmmaker established his reputation as a top director with the box office hit *Close Encounters of the Third Kind* (1977), a film in which Spielberg explored human contact with *extraterrestrials* (aliens). He was inspired by the events surrounding Flight 19—one of the greatest mysteries of the Bermuda Triangle—when he wrote the script for this science-fiction film. In the movie, Spielberg shows the disappearance of Flight 19 as having been the result of an alien abduction.

Frustrated Rescue

After losing contact with Flight 19, authorities at the Fort Lauderdale base ordered a Martin Mariner seaplane to take off and begin a rescue operation. With a crew of 13, the seaplane sent several routine messages as it took off and began the flight to the area where it was believed that the five TBM Avengers had crash landed in the sea. After a few minutes, however, all radio communications from the Martin Mariner ceased. A nearby ship later reported that it had observed an explosion in the air at approximately the time the seaplane ceased communicating with the base. Thus, this flight has been added to the list of odd crashes, disappearances, and mishaps that seem to plague the Bermuda Triangle. In reality, the Martin Mariner had a poor safety reputation and were known among pilots as "flying gas tanks."

MARTIN MARINER
A seaplane (above), identical to the one that exploded while searching for Flight 19, remains afloat shortly after crashing on take-off in 1943.

what devilry is taking place there." Another committee member admitted to the press that "we couldn't even make a good guess as to what happened." But, the investigators agreed that any number of things could have gone wrong, including the failure of navigation instruments, failures in radio communications, sudden bad weather, and the approaching nightfall.

An official report blamed errors by Lieutenant Taylor for the loss of the flight. More than 50 years later, British *aviation* (flying) specialist Phil Gilles listened to the flight radio recordings from that day. He concluded that Lieutenant Taylor was not in the appropriate mental state to lead the maneuvers, especially since the rest of the squadron pilots were new and rather inexperienced.

It is certainly possible that a strong tail wind pushed the squadron off course so that Lieutenant Taylor became confused when he should have veered northwest to begin the return to base. His radio communications make it clear that the compass on his TBM Avenger seemed to be malfunctioning. Without a

compass to navigate, Lieutenant Taylor may have relied on certain landmarks, especially known islands in the region, to gain a sense of direction. This could have caused problems. From the air, it is easy to mistake one island for another. Lieutenant Taylor may have been incorrect about his exact location in the flight after mistaking the elongated shape of Great Abaco island for that of Grand Bahama island or even the Florida Keys, and taken a wrong turn. Once he lost his bearings, it seems Lieutenant Taylor also lost the calm he needed to recover control of the situation. The inexperienced pilots who made up the rest of the squadron had no choice but to follow their commander into oblivion.

The Ghost Ships of the Bermuda Triangle

Sometimes ships are found drifting in the Bermuda Triangle without any sign of the crew. Experts are baffled by the mysteries presented by these "ghost ships."

Shipwrecks occur in modern times despite the fact that safety on the oceans has greatly improved since the time of sail-powered ships. At times, small pleasure boats, yachts, fishing vessels, and even large cargo ships weighing many tons are lost to storms in the vast ocean. Even today, ships occasionally become *derelict* (unkept) and are found drifting aimlessly, with little evidence as to what became of the crew. Some people believe the Bermuda Triangle has more than its fair share of such "ghost ships."

The most famous discovery of a ghost ship, the *Mary Celeste* in 1872, is still incorrectly associated with the Bermuda Triangle even as *skeptics* (nonbelievers) have pointed out that this ship was found thousands of miles away from the region. Yet, many other ghost ships have been found abandoned in the Bermuda Triangle. These include the *Rosalie* (1840), the *Carrol A. Deering* (1921), the *Rubicon* (1944), the *City Belle* (1946), and the *Connemara IV* (1955), all found drifting in perfect condition. In all instances the ship's crew and passengers were gone, never to be seen again.

One of the most mysterious events involved the English ship *Ellen Austin* (1881), which encountered an abandoned *schooner* (two-masted ship) in good condition in the Atlantic. The captain put some of his crew onboard the deserted schooner, and both vessels continued sailing side by side, heading for the nearest port. Later, the ships were separated by fog for several days. When the fog had finally lifted, the entire crew on the schooner had again vanished.

Although storms are the most common cause for the loss of ships, stories of the Bermuda Triangle "ghost ships" have inspired some of the more fantastic explanations from the most fervent devotees of the legends surrounding the region. For example, in his book *Limbo of the Lost* (1969), author John. W. Spencer proposed that the crews had been abducted onto a spaceship by *extraterrestrials* (aliens).

THE SHIP "BLANCHE CASTLE" IN A WHIRLWIND.—SEE PAGE 354.

OCEAN HAZARDS

Sudden storms in the waters of the Bermuda Triangle are dangerous to ships and crews.

GHOST SHIP

Abandoned derelict ships that remain afloat are found drifting throughout the oceans of the world. Some of the most well-known of these "ghost ships" were found in the waters of the Bermuda Triangle.

Navigation Instruments

From the very beginning, the history of sailing has been linked to developments in *navigation* (direction finding) instruments. Ancient sailors used simple observation of the sun and stars, and from these early methods, there was a steady progression of scientific development of navigation technology.

Safer Sailing

Bermuda Triangle investigators are accustomed to looking back at instances of ships disappearing without logical explanation as far back as the 1500's, when navigation on the high seas was still rather crude. However, shipwrecks from the 1800's and 1900's cannot be examined in the same way, since knowledge of navigation was much greater compared to earlier times. The technology used by ships in modern times allows much greater control over ships. Today, sailing is much safer and the disappearance of ships without a clear cause is very rare indeed.

SEXTANT

This device (above) appeared in the 1700's to replace the astrolabe and measure angles between the sun, the North Star, and the horizon. If you knew the time, you could determine your position with some precision.

OLD COMPASS

The traditional compass (above) indicates magnetic north with a needle. The fact that it did not indicate geographic north, located to the east of the magnetic pole, induced errors.

NAUTICAL CHART

Portolans, the medieval charts used to recognize coastlines, became shipping charts in the 1400's, when sailors set out across the open sea. This chart (left) from the late 1500's shows the Caribbean and the Gulf of Mexico.

MODERN COMPASS

By incorporating electronic technology, the modern compass (right) can correct the error that occurs between magnetic north and geographic north.

RADAR

Radar (acronym for *Ra*dio *D*etection *A*nd *R*anging) caused a revolution in navigation after it was first used toward the middle of the 1900's. It is an electronic system that gives off electromagnetic waves to measure distances, directions, and the speed of objects, such as boats and airplanes. It remains an important instrument on ships and airplanes, as radar can also identify weather events.

Foucault's gyroscope

Invented in 1852 by French scientist Jean-Bernard Léon Foucault—who also invented the pendulum—for a demonstration of the Earth's rotation, the gyroscope was not originally created as a navigation instrument. Foucault realized that it could well serve to indicate north if the movements of the base were fixed. The device was also useful for reducing the rolling movements of ships.

QUADRANT

This device (above) was used from the 1400's to determine position by measuring the distance between the horizon and the sun or the North Star, but it needed two people to operate it.

ASTROLABE

Created by Greek astronomers around 200 B.C., the astrolabe (above) is a circle that lets you locate the stars and determine position and time of day. It was widely used until the invention of the sextant.

CROSS-STAFF OR JACOB'S STAFF

Developed in the 1300's to make astronomical measurements, the cross-staff (right) was a strip of wood that slid on a stick. To measure the latitude, you had to point the device at the sun or the North Star and then move the crossbar to line up with the horizon.

GPS

Available commercially beginning in the 1990's (left), Global Positioning System (GPS) devices use a complex system of satellites to give the precise location of a ship, airplane, or even an automobile or person.

Clinton Macomb

What Happened to the USS *Cyclops*?

The huge ship vanished on a routine voyage nearly a century ago. Despite many theories proposed to explain the loss, the disappearance of the USS *Cyclops* remains one of the greatest mysteries of the Bermuda Triangle.

Those who believe in the the presence of supernatural forces in Bermuda Triangle point to the unexplained disappearance in 1918 of the *collier* (cargo ship) USS *Cyclops*, somewhere between Barbados and Virginia as proof that such forces are at work in the region. At 542 feet (165 meters) in length, the steel-hulled *Cyclops* was one of the largest vessels in the world at the time. Even today, underwater adventurers search for this vessel in hopes of discovering its fate.

On February 15, 1918, with Captain George W. Worley and 308 passengers and crew on board, the *Cyclops* sailed from Rio de Janeiro, carrying a load of manganese ore destined for Baltimore, with no scheduled stops in between. However, on March 3, the ship made an unexpected stop at Barbados, in the West Indies, where engine problems were reported. The ship set off the next day. However, the *Cyclops* never arrived in Baltimore, and no trace has been seen since.

A search was begun once the ship was reported overdue. Since World War I was still raging in Europe, many people suspected that the *Cyclops* may have been torpedoed by a German submarine or blown up after striking a *mine* (an underwater explosive device used to sink ships). However, the *Cyclops* did not send a SOS, and there were no reports of enemy submarines along the route. The weather was known to be stormy in the region, but the *Cyclops* did not broadcast any radio messages suggesting difficulties. The ship's cargo of highly flammable manganese ore raised the possibility of an explosion or catastrophic fire, but such an occurrence would have left bodies and wreckage scattered across the ocean.

The leading theory as to the fate of the *Cyclops* is that the enormous ship *foundered* (filled with water) and capsized in rough seas during stormy weather en route to Baltimore. However, many Bermuda Triangle proponents find it hard to believe that such a large ship could remain lost for so long. They argue that until divers discover the sunken wreck of the USS *Cyclops*, mysterious causes for the ship's disappearance cannot be completely ruled out.

The USS *Cyclops*

"One of the Sea's Most Baffling Mysteries." This is how the disappearance of the cargo ship the USS *Cyclops* (above), one of the largest vessels in the world at the time, was described by Bermuda Triangle investigators. The *Cyclops* sank in 1918 somewhere between Barbados and Virginia. Throughout history, shipwrecks are known to be common in the region, but wreckage from such disasters is almost always found. Yet no trace of the enormous *Cyclops* has been located after nearly a century.

SHIP REMAINS
A retired sailor displays objects recovered from the many shipwrecks that have occurred off the coast of Cape Hatteras, North Carolina, on the route of the USS *Cyclops*.

Malaysia Airlines Flight 370

With all the modern communication and navigation technology available today, how is it still possible for ships and airplanes to go missing?

Many ships, airplanes, and people have disappeared in the section of the Atlantic Ocean known as the Bermuda Triangle. However, the majority of these disappearances have occurred between about the 1500's and 1960. Today, with modern communication and *navigation* (direction-finding) technology, including radar, cellular telephones, and the Global Positioning System (GPS), the complete disappearance of a large ship or airplane seems unthinkable. But on March 8, 2014, Malaysia Airlines Flight 370 vanished on a routine overnight flight between Kuala Lumpur, Malaysia, and Beijing, China.

Within days, an international media storm occurred as experts and amateurs alike speculated on the whereabouts of the Boeing 777 airliner and the 239 passengers and crew on board. Like many of the disappearances in the Bermuda Triangle, Flight 370 did not transmit any distress call. The last radio message from the pilot suggested no difficulties with weather or equipment.

Radar tracking during the early portion of the flight showed that the airplane made an unexpected turn towards the Indian Ocean, in the opposite direction of its destination. Over the Indian Ocean, the airplane was no longer tracked by radar. Other evidence suggests the airplane flew south for several hours before it disappeared. After an exhaustive international search, no wreckage or other traces of Flight 370 have been found.

The loss of the airplane, and the media frenzy that followed, showed the tension between trust in an all-seeing technology and the near-impossibility of locating a plane in the vastness of an ocean. Despite theories involving hijackings and secret landings, most experts concluded that the airplane crashed in the Indian Ocean. However, some people have speculated that Flight 370 fell victim to the mysterious forces that may operate in another "infernal triangle" on the opposite side of Earth from the Bermuda Triangle.

ANOTHER LOST FLIGHT

Malaysia Airlines Flight 370 vanished on March 8, 2014. No trace of the Boeing 777 airliner has been found. Information from satellites (below) shows the airplane made an unexpected turn and flew south over the vast Indian Ocean.

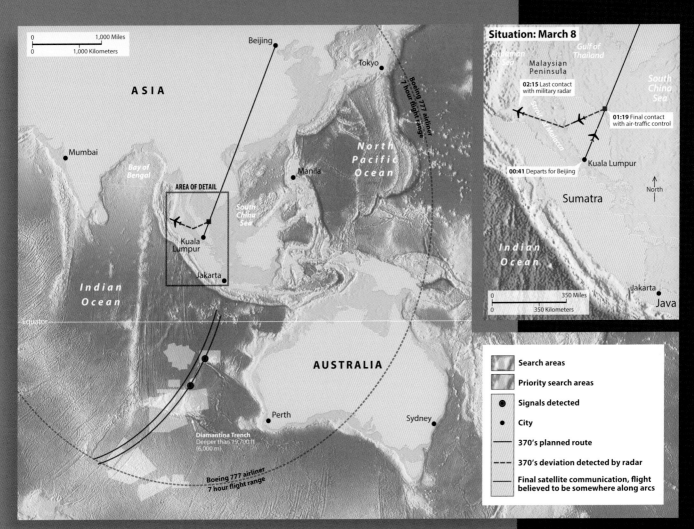

Situation: March 8

Andaman Sea
Gulf of Thailand
Malaysian Peninsula
02:15 Last contact with military radar
South China Sea
Strait of Malacca
01:19 Final contact with air-traffic control
00:41 Departs for Beijing
Kuala Lumpur
North
Sumatra
Indian Ocean
Jakarta
Java

0 — 350 Miles
0 — 350 Kilometers

0 — 1,000 Miles
0 — 1,000 Kilometers

Beijing
Tokyo
ASIA
North Pacific Ocean
Boeing 777 airliner 7 hour flight range
Mumbai
Bay of Bengal
AREA OF DETAIL
South China Sea
Manila
Kuala Lumpur
Jakarta
Indian Ocean
Equator
AUSTRALIA
Perth
Sydney
Diamantina Trench
Deeper than 19,700 ft (6,000 m)
Boeing 777 airliner 7 hour flight range

	Search areas
	Priority search areas
●	Signals detected
•	City
——	370's planned route
- - -	370's deviation detected by radar
——	Final satellite communication, flight believed to be somewhere along arcs

WORLD BOOK map; image provided by National Oceanic and Atmospheric Administration, National Geophysical Data Center
Sources: Malaysian Government, Australian Maritime Safety Authority

Avoiding More Mysteries

Since its use began in the 1990's, the Global Positioning System (GPS) has dramatically improved the navigation of ships and aircraft that cross the ocean and has aided in finding their location in the event of an emergency.

GPS

GPS (Global Positioning System) is a method of *navigation* (science of figuring out position) by satellite by which the position of a ship, aircraft, or even a person can be determined with great precision, at virtually any place on the planet. Since the introduction of this technology—and others like it, such as the Russian Glonass or the European Galileo—the number of disappearances in the Bermuda Triangle and other trouble spots of the oceans has diminished. It has simply become more difficult to get lost!

When things do go bad, GPS helps rescue ships and aircraft locate the distressed vessel.

1 TRIANGULATION

To determine the position of an object, GPS employs *triangulation*: determining the distance between the object and three satellites, and using three numbers to calculate the position.

2 DISTANCES

The GPS receiver captures the exact position issued by a satellite, which establishes distance by calculating the time the signals take to reach the receiver.

24 SATELLITES

The GPS system uses 24 satellites that cover the entire Earth at an altitude of around 87,205 feet (26,580 meters).

MEASUREMENT

All positions (latitude, longitude, and time) are calculated from a minimum of 4 of the 24 available satellites.

COMMUNICATIONS CENTER

The base for the GPS on Earth is equipped with powerful satellite dishes to receive signals from orbiting satellites.

Highly diverse receivers

The GPS terminals or receivers indicate the user's current position. There are receivers for cars, boats, airplanes, even for people walking, and they are incorporated into many makes of mobile phones.

Digital Mapping

The GPS global *navigation* (direction-finding) system would have been impossible without the development of digital *cartography* (mapping), which is incorporated in nearly all navigation systems of modern ships. The image on the left shows the GPS navigation screen from the Russian icebreaker *Kapitan Khlebnikov*, in which a fragment of the coast of Antarctica is identifiable.

3 SYNCHRONIZATION

All the satellite systems are perfectly *synchronized* (kept in time) with each other and with the communications center by means of accurate clocks.

4 POSITION

The receiver repeats step 2 with two other satellites to determine the exact triangulation.

5 CORRECTION

A fourth satellite is used to refine the measurements of the first three and confirm the position.

The GPS system has a margin of error of less than 8 feet (2.5 meters) although there is also differential GPS, which guarantees precision to within 3 feet (1 meter), through the use of a fixed point of reference (below) that provides great accuracy to the system.

SYNCHRONIZED SIGNALS

The communications center receives the synchronized signals from all the satellites and sends them to the user.

GPS terminals on ships look similar to those now common in automobiles.

Are There Other "Infernal Areas" of the World?

The Bermuda Triangle is not the only place on Earth with a history of disappearing ships and aircraft. Many other regions, such as the Devil's Sea south of Japan, have similar reputations.

Even though the name seen on maps and nautical charts is the Philippine Sea, this western region of the Pacific Ocean south of Japan is known to the local fishermen by such fearsome names as the Devil's Sea or the Dragon's Triangle. This portion of the Pacific is, aside from the Bermuda Triangle, one of the most well known of the so-called "*infernal* (cursed) triangles," regions that seem to be plagued by mysterious forces capable of terrorizing fishermen, mariners, and pilots alike.

In the Devil's Sea, just like the Bermuda Triangle, there have been reports of disappearing boats and airplanes and encounters with ghost ships. Supposed encounters with *extraterrestrial* (alien) ships and instances of space-time warping have also been reported (although scientific experts consider accounts of these latter incidents to be highly questionable). Upon closer examination, however, the region is decidedly less mysterious than claimed.

MASSIVE DISAPPEARANCES

Investigator Charles Berlitz, widely known for his studies on the Bermuda Triangle, published the essay *The Dragon's Triangle* in 1989. Here, he claimed that five large Japanese military ships disappeared with more than 700 people on board between 1952 and 1954. According to Berlitz, the Japanese government sent a ship with more than 100 experts to investigate these occurrences, but this ship also disappeared. As a result, Japanese authorities decided to classify the area as extremely dangerous.

However, Bermuda Triangle investigator Larry Kusche points out several exaggerations by Berlitz. Kusche maintains that the Japanese government has never declared the area south of Japan as particularly dangerous. The five missing ships referred to by Berlitz were, in reality, fishing boats that were shipwrecked during the many storms common in that region. The investigation ship Berlitz mentions was actually studying not those disappearances, but the activity of an underwater volcano called *Myojin-sho*. The eruption of this volcano sank the ship.

Upon closer examination, Kusche has found that the Devil's Sea is decidedly less mysterious than many have claimed. Might the same be true of the Bermuda Triangle?

Zones of Mystery

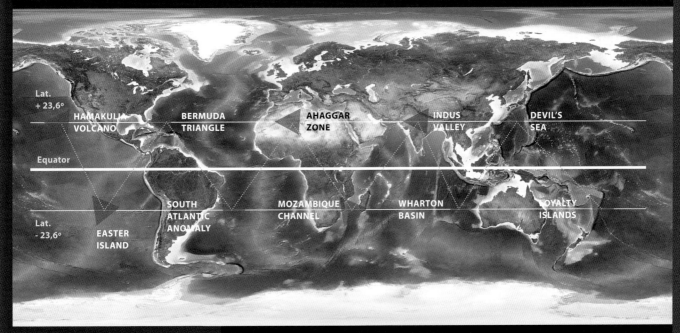

Lat. + 23,6°

HAMAKULIA VOLCANO

BERMUDA TRIANGLE

AHAGGAR ZONE

INDUS VALLEY

DEVIL'S SEA

Equator

Lat. - 23,6°

EASTER ISLAND

SOUTH ATLANTIC ANOMALY

MOZAMBIQUE CHANNEL

WHARTON BASIN

LOYALTY ISLANDS

The Vile Vortices

Scottish author Ivan T. Sanderson published the article "The Twelve Devil's Graveyards Around the World" in a 1972 issue of *Saga* magazine, in which he outlined his theory of the *Vile Vortices*, twelve regions where the disappearances of airplanes and ships, as well as other *paranormal* (outside the bounds of normal) activity, have been supposedly recorded. (A *vortex* [plural *vortices*] is a swirling mass of water that pulls in nearby objects.) Among these vortices are the Bermuda Triangle and the Devil's Sea. (The polar regions are included in the 12 zones, but are not shown on the map above.) It is surprising that these vortices include some areas on dry land, such as the Indus Valley, in India, Africa's Sahara Desert, and Antarctica. Nearly all scientific experts doubt Sanderson's claims.

The Mystery of Lake Ontario

The approximate area of 95,000 square miles (246,050 square kilometers) of Lake Ontario, one of North America's Great Lakes, is one of the largest bodies of fresh water on the planet. Due to its size, Lake Ontario has weather patterns similar to those found in the ocean, including fierce storms that have caused many shipwrecks and disappearances.

Some investigators claim that these occurrences are not due to weather alone. They have identified what they believe to be three mysterious zones in Lake Ontario: the so-called Marysburgh Vortex, situated in the northeast part of the lake, where two-thirds of the recorded disappearances have taken place; the Sophiasburgh Triangle, 55 miles (88 kilometers) west, where a supposed variation in the Earth's magnetic field alters the proper functioning of compasses, leading to accidents in stormy or foggy weather; and the Lake Michigan Triangle, well known after two disappearances: that of a coal freighter in 1937 and that of a Northwest Orient Airlines flight in 1950, which vanished without a trace with 58 people on board.

FEATURELESS SEAS
Viewed from space, beneath
scattered clouds in this view,
the region of the Atlantic Ocean
known as the Bermuda Triangle
appears as a featureless
expanse of water.

Places to See and Visit

OTHER PLACES OF INTEREST

NATIONAL MUSEUM OF BERMUDA

SANDYS, BERMUDA ISLANDS

Discovered in 1505 by Spanish sailor Juan de Bermúdez, from whom the area gets its name, the Bermuda islands were colonized in the 1600's after a fleet led by Admiral George Somers foundered among the islands and the crew found shelter on them. At what once was the Royal Naval Dockyard, at Sandys, on the far west side of the largest island, is the Bermuda Maritime Museum. The exhibits cover five hundred years of sailing history.

NAVAL AIR STATION MUSEUM

FORT LAUDERDALE, FLORIDA

The Naval Air Station at Fort Lauderdale, Florida, is the base from which the tragic squadron of Flight 19 took off. The squadron's disappearance in 1945 and the following investigations led in part to the creation of the Bermuda Triangle mystery. One of the base's original buildings houses an interesting naval air museum, which holds documents, books, photographs, objects, and naval art connected to the area's history, in addition to material linked to the mystery of Flight 19.

MEL FISHER MARITIME MUSEUM

KEY WEST, FLORIDA

On the island of Key West, south of Florida, stands the Mel Fisher Museum, dedicated to this famous treasure hunter, known for his 1985 discovery of the wreck of the Spanish *galleon* (large, high fighting ship of multiple decks and large sails) *Nuestra Señora de Atocha*, which sank in 1622. The museum houses jewels, coins, and many similar objects recovered by the diver.

Bahamas

NASSAU

Located on the small island of New Providence, the capital of the Bahamas is home to approximately 70 percent of the island chain's population. Named in 1695, Nassau retains its colonial English atmosphere, and has many sites of interest related to the sea. The most notable is the Pirates Museum, with recreations of a 1700's shipping wharf, including a tavern typical of that time and the pirate ship *Revenge*.

BIMINI

This district, made up of two larger islands, is famous for the so-called "Bimini Road," an odd underwater rock formation that looks as if it is human made. Some have claimed that the rocks represent massive building from the legendary lost continent of Atlantis. However, scientists believe the rock formation resulted from natural means.

THE TONGUE OF THE OCEAN

The shallow waters around the Bahamas are an underwater paradise for divers. But not far off the coast of Andros Island, lies the so-called "Tongue of the Ocean," a deep underwater trench that is home to an enormous variety of sea creatures.

Bimini Road

Built by people and later submerged, or simply a natural rock formation, the Bimini Road never fails to impress. These stretches of aligned rock are found near North Bimini island and are easy to access, even by inexperienced divers.

GRAVEYARD OF THE ATLANTIC

CAPE HATTERAS, NORTH CAROLINA

Located on the eastern coast of North Carolina, Cape Hatteras is a strip of land that projects outward into the Atlantic Ocean. It is one of the key *navigational* (direction finding) landmarks on the U.S. coast. Hatteras is home to the interesting Graveyard of the Atlantic Museum, which details the cape's maritime history. The cape itself consists of a sandy bank connecting to firmer ground on the coast. This bank has been the site of numerous shipwrecks throughout the ages. The museum contains objects recovered from these shipwrecks and has interesting exhibits on the many warships and pirate ships that once sailed the local waters.

Glossary

Archipelago— A group of many islands.

Aviation— The art or science of operating and navigating aircraft.

Bathyscaph— A deep-sea vessel used for underwater exploration.

Calm— An absence of wind or motion, particularly on the ocean.

Collier— A large cargo ship for carrying coal or other bulk material.

Clairvoyant— A person supposedly having the power of seeing or knowing about things in the future or that are out of sight.

Derelict— A ship abandoned and afloat at sea.

Extraterrestrial— Alien. A being from a planet other than Earth.

Galleon— A large fighting ship, usually with three or four decks and square sails.

GPS— Global Positioning System, a worldwide system that uses radio signals broadcast by orbiting satellites to determine the position of a ship, airplane, or other vehicle.

Gulf Stream— A strong, warm ocean current that flows out of the Gulf of Mexico, north along the coast of the United States and Newfoundland, and northeast across the Atlantic toward Europe.

Infernal— Cursed, evil, or diabolical.

Linguist— A person who studies the history and structure of language.

Mine— An explosive device put under water to sink ships.

Navigation— The science of determining the position and course of a ship or aircraft.

Paranormal— Outside normal perception or knowledge.

Schooner— A ship with two or more masts and front and back sails.

Skeptic— A person who questions the truth of theories.

Sonar— A device for detecting and locating objects under water by the reflection of sound waves.

Synchronize— To move or take place at the same time and exactly together.

Triangulation— To survey, measure, and map out (a region) by dividing (it) into triangles and measuring their angles and sides.

Tsunami— A large oceanic wave caused by a submarine earthquake or volcanic eruption.

UFO— An unidentified flying object.

For Further Information

Books

Belanger, Jeff, and Stephen Marchesi. *The Mysteries of the Bermuda Triangle.* New York: Grosset & Dunlap, 2010. Print.

Ganeri, Anita, and David West. *Lost in the Bermuda Triangle and Other Mysteries.* New York: Rosen Central, 2012. Print.

Hayes, Amy, ed. *Beliefs, Rituals, and Symbols of the Modern World.* New York: Cavendish Square, 2015. Print.

Zuchora-Walske, Christine, and W. Sean Chamberlin. *The Bermuda Triangle.* Minneapolis: ABDO, 2012. Print.

Websites

"Bermuda Triangle." *History.com.* A&E Television Networks, 2015. Web. 11 Feb. 2015.

"Bermuda Triangle Mystery." *National Geographic Channel.* National Geographic, 2015. Web. 25 Feb. 2015.

"Drain the Bermuda Triangle." *National Geographic Channel.* National Geographic, 2015. Web. 24 Feb. 2015.

"What Is the Bermuda Triangle?" *National Ocean Service.* NOAA, 4 Jan. 2010. Web. 24 Feb. 2015.

Index

Acknowledgments

Pictures:

© Age Fotostock

© Alamy Images

AP Images

© Barry M. Schwortz Collection, STERA, Inc.

© Corbis Images

© Dr. Leen Ritmeyer

© Getty Images

© Granger

© Kris Simoens

© L. Garlaschelli

Library of Congress

© Mitchell Library, State Library of New South Wales

© National Geographic Stock

© Other Images

© Petaqui

© Sacred Destinations Images

© Shutterstock

© Topfoto

© Mitchell Library, State Library of New South Wales